too Many Words

JAMIE SHAW

Paperback: 978-1-960861-24-5
eBook: 978-1-960861-23-8
Library of Congress Control Number: 2023910393

This is a work of nonfiction.

SWEETSPIRE LITERATURE
— MANAGEMENT —

Table of Contents

[O N E]

Lily Song

Yes! Slender, slim, though quite unthin—
As she thus ever was—
When how her black jeans hugged her pins
Would drop my jaws—because!
She knew I knew her forest-fleece
Pullover came along
To wake my senses, win my peace—
In combination strong!
When then, in list, I took a risk,
No matter what the cost—
(I urged to splurge, to purge my surge,
And count no second lost—)
As, mooching up, my trembling cup
Of silver in her spell,
Too weak to find resistance meek,
I puckered on a distant cheek—
A streaming, teaming, piquant, chic
Intention to belong—
As, fond her wand upon my frond,
In lily song I fell!

[T W O]

Thou, Whom I Call Champ

The boy in blue, who wanted to
Be naval from the start,
Art one to be so pinioned through
His holy, holy heart…
If I, O Chris, were thine to judge,
For that I wouldn't thee,
My love for thee would not be poor,
The moor so slippery!
No better man doth tread the turf—
If time have tide to tell
That we are friends, to tread the surf,
So let me be as well!
So here am I, grey-green the sea
Deflecting Suns I stole
From thine, too bright, inherently
A better shot at goal…
A fleck of brown is left, I think,
Still should I speak again
With thee, I guess it might be pink—
Thine only to explain!

[THREE]

Emma

Matchless beauty, spirit, heart, release
For me is loath—
If you should stop, I'd ever cease
My Hippocratic Oath—
And light a fire, brandish peace
Especial, for us both—
Howbeit grander expertise
Is neither here, nor wroth…
No break-and-enter, no disdain
Nonsensical—of yore
We'd turn our love on Key Biscayne
To ashes, folk and lore,
As I, ascending, lost to pain,
Look down upon a shore
Far, far away—from which to gain
The Sun begins to thaw.

[FOUR]

How Many Roses

How many roses do I
Bestow, to see you smile
In canopies or clusters,
And make you last a while?

So long as I shall breathe,
Your love is in my heart—
Bewitching to believe,
Though tyrants would us part,
That restoration prospers,
Such, even if we lose,
Regeneration's loss purrs
Creation, as we cruise!

[F I V E]

Song In My Heart

Her beauty spot, bedaubèd on
Perfection's little nose,
Is brown—so pink the raw bed on
Her canvas someone chose…

So let us wonder, through the days,
If love have time to lose—
If she will be here yesterday,
Or vanish, like the news…

He doesn't wish to live a lie,
To live without her love
Enveloping the evening sky
Still high, so high above—

And so, she scampers here in lieu
Of fenced-in concrete lawns,
Where hearts of blood cheer much ado
In sunshine God adorns.

[SIX]

Ruby Love

Give purity a miss?
I recollect your name!
If you're denying this
Is nuancing the same
Occasion for my bliss,
I reapportion blame
To modesty—for truly tis
Love's whisper, not a game!

How many dreams of hamlets
Encircle you at night?
Though raging Roger Ramjets
Catch fire at your sight—
A druid apt to damn whets
His sickle for the fight,
Before a Paschal lamb lets
Your sunshine, as of might

Surge fifteen trillion miles
To reach a foreign eye,
Which, winking at your trials,
Would love, and live, and die!

[SEVEN]

Lily of My Evergreen Valley

Goodness gracious! Loving thee
I slept upon eternity,
Dreaming in my waking hours,
Drinking rose-hip tea and flowers,
Soaking up my timeless youth
Into some kind of extant ruth—
To render storm and wind defenceless,
And ones that batter me, immense less...

Thy spirit is a wave of sand
Left motionless at my command,
To see prismatic rays collect
The sunlight popinjays inspect,
Our faith in love was once in hope
Felicity's kaleidoscope—
To woo the woman in my soul
Makes yesterday effete, and whole.

[EIGHT]

Edible Eve

Edible Eve, naked and ripe,
Thought Adam not good enough—didn't she now!
Might he've been happy he wasn't her type—
To worship Godiva, instead of a cow?

What, sex with the Devil, that asp with the bite,
Was that what an innocent man ought endure?
So what if his oxygen wasn't as bright
As, channelling darkness, his ozone got fewer!

O Fashion Madonna, yes, what does it bring
When loyalty languishing, marrow and bone,
Thinks primeval jungle's not somewhere to sing
Karaoke upon his unlimited phone!

[NINE]

In Concert

So, optimal woman, so pert, hip, and one
For ducking and weaving—how can it be true?
However I put it down, rings can be run
Around your contenders, as much as I do

Remember the cactuses poking, in fun,
The silicone slippers our principals slew—
If I were your monkey, would you be my nun
And rue all the jellyfish nobody knew?

Well, you've gotta answer—love isn't a game,
Chess isn't my wife, though I'd like her to be:
Caïssa, above every other a name
To carry the day and re-settle the sea

Quick, open, and beautiful, not quite the same
As you once beheld a poor zealot, whose plea
May tickle some feathers for fealty's dame,
Who he'd have you know is for weal—tis she!

[TEN]

Ashton

By goodness she is loved,
By kindness she is graced:
As chocolate goes with coconut,
As innocence is chaste,

She knows the grace of love inside,
The freedom of its peace—
In purity a lion's pride
Will sacrifice, to cease...

The sound of love is circular,
Once, entering a door,
Lines far from perpendicular,
In waves upon a shore,

Create the sound of seeming
So lovelily unknown—
A crystal ocean fond of streaming
Rivers she has sewn.

[ELEVEN]

Rhonda

A tender strawberry, lovely blonde
At sixteen still—a star
Here twinkling on, so doubly fond
Of Papa's good Mama…

Man but a boy cannot elude
The waves that break her lines—
To think of her, yet not intrude
On fantasies of vines

And rose-hip jam, on fresh white bread,
Salvation's only gift:
Where is the venom, having bled
That cosmic, *seismic* shift,

And, smiling still, creating life
In mimicry of sand—
The salt that washes tang, in strife,
Is her confetti, fanned!

[TWELVE]

Marilyn

How lovelily the sky awakes—
Caffes latte, 'nana cakes
And little woofs 'n' pats 'n' purrs,
In palaces, by woods 'n' lakes…

Sticks 'n' snakes are not for us,
Nor hers—a momentary thought occurs:
To matronise the universe,
On horses' hooves and knightly spurs

We're welcoming beyond a door—
When, rollin' up, then rollin' down,
Her leaves are forest green or brown,
So sent below to go to show

That she's no kitten to ignore
When, once awake, the music snores
Mid little ones—for whom no chores
Would rake remains up into wars, till laws
Should cease—in peace—Piscean scores
His love devotes to twenty-four.

[THIRTEEN]

Flathead, Whiting, Cat

The roller-door rolled up.
A smidgen—just enough:
A turtle dove, a pigeon
The taxi-drivers stuff…

She's hiding in the living room—
Living, down to her:
The purest being anywhere
That coos, or breathes—to purr

And ever, in my heart,
Till sunset did abide,
To rise again—not open wide,
To stop again, to start,
But live eternal—

Where is time
Except here in our soul?
And, warming up,
A silver dime
The nickel in her bowl.

[FOURTEEN]

Melissa

So soft as any flower
Is sweet for any jam,
Is gentle as a little honey
Marinating lamb—

Is mooing like a kangaroo—
Something in her pouch
Is putting peas together with
Potatoes on a couch…

Where did I put her mirror?
You're hearing into how
Each moment is a memory—
Earwitnesses kow-tow

To be the tiger in the parks,
The lions in the zoo—
If words could capture inner sparks,
I'd be there, just for you!

[FIFTEEN]

James

A pomegranate, on the house
Of love, infused with me:
I'll put the kettle on—a mouse
Just will, or won't, be free…

Young man, how do you stay so young?
You're nigh on thirty-nine!
And clinical, and senior, sprung
Like mice—they say that wine

If old, is in a bottle new,
A little left of odd:
Were we but cousins, peas who grew
Up in a distant pod,

I'd take a sip—where is my jar
Of tablets keeping pace?
Instead of cranberry in a bar,
You're winding up my case!

[S I X T E E N]

Oz Chess Art

Forks and prelates, skewers, pins—
Let's eat a prawn or two!
Piscean pizza, no mistakes,
Though lessons from your brew
Are keeping clean good forty years
Of friendship, on a cob—
Are *you* my dreamboat?
Hooks and sneers
Prepare to weave and bob!

And boats are ever feminine,
A pleonastic rhyme
Would make of us a gender snob,
And Port my jelly wine…

How many moves are our reward,
How many tries that mate?
I'm sitting on defence, Good Lord,
But *szeretlek* makes eight!

[SEVENTEEN]

Ashtonier

One is, or one just isn't
The friend in every star,
The light in every prism,
Octavian trala!

A chicken wouldn't cross her way
If she were not a hen
A-putting all her moss away
To gather up a pen:

Remember, love, my heart's a flame,
Evincing it for thee—
My life with thee much less a game,
Befriending hope for three...

Loquacious, though thou call my bluff,
Insidious my clue—
No way, Hosanna, one's enough,
Germane to me, and you!

[EIGHTEEN]

Jacinta So Winsome

To love, or not to love may be
Another question—answer soon!
On set collision course with thee,
This tear of Jupiter's a rune…
So, what'll be her quip—a basket
Case should pull in horns off-tune?
If love's a lucky dip, to ask it
Smacks of August, lost in June!
And wherefore art thou, anyway,
Intent on holding clammy hands?
To Gods in love, as many say,
The pudding in the proof commands!
If planets in the sky abound,
Play with old socks and worn-out shoes—
If you want dogs and cats around,
Best pray for litters, minus blues!

[NINETEEN]

Hymn to Her

She's caring—let me give her one
Or other, to enclose
Succession to the living Sun:
Ubiquities of rose...

Zoology's theology's
Philosophies in times
I ask myself—apologies
She's locking into crimes!
Caress the dame, impress the myrrh,
Be frank in sense, resign—
To groom a womb, a golden burr
Left languishing in wine!

Yet I have been abominable—
Hang this cross of hurt!
Where were you, Adam—in a stable,
Giving love a spurt?
I think I thought I heard you damn
The day a faun forlorn
Was torn from Ma'am, just like the lamb
Begotten into scorn.

[T W E N T Y]

The Passing of The Winter

Peace there be in little ones:
Cousin, cousine, our daughters, sons—
Company we may replace,
But not the look upon the face
Of Harriet, or Kevin, Max,
In flesh and clothing—melting wax
Takes fire and a wick that burns
Away the lessons history learns...

Winners? Losers? God's in charge
Of Chevrolets in your garage,
Of puppetries, albeit will
May tap upon your windowsill...

How do you do, my heart of gold,
Humility at once so bold?
Where art thou gone, the one that shone
On stages every night—anon,
If thou shouldst grant me twenty years,
I'd rise above, to cry for tears!

[TWENTY-ONE]

Beauteous, Gorgeous, And Lovely

Thou, my precious, art
So much more than a gem—
So much more than a cartwheel
For my REM…

Thou art my truly magical,
A miracle, a mage—
If mages can be tragical,
Then let me be your sage!

God, grant me wishes, let them be
Your lovely flowing locks,
Your gorgeousness, in total—see
How beautiful it rocks!

And when tomorrow lets us hope
For other ones to come,
I'd slither on your slippery slope—
In handing you my thumb!

[TWENTY-TWO]

Awesome, Lovely, True, And Taken

What loveliness, what truth, what style—
Lending it to me a while!
Just to see your spirit smile
Is worth it:
Like a little child,
Yet somehow now much more a man
Than when your suns and moons began
To treat me with your awesome "can!"—
To see me soar, then see me land!

And so, we're eating quiche today—
We'd have it any other way
If we could knot the stars to stay
Just where they are—
To shine like clay!

[T W E N T Y - T H R E E]

Sonnenuntergang

Um diese Jahreszeit,
Die Tage nicht zu lang,
Gezwitscher weit und breit,
Gelausche und Gesang
Kommen mir zunutze,
Und das nicht ohne die
Gehange zum Geputze
Innewohner wie
Georg und dessen Gattin,
Die Liebe offen sah'n
In Feldern, die gestatten
Essen und Gewahr'n.

[TWENTY-FOUR]

Sonnenaufgang

In diesem Leben gibt es
Liebe und, ich hoff,
Muße und Erbeben—
Soweit ich mich ersoff!
Kannst du, in der Ferne,
Bienen trinken seh'n?
Das Flüstern ihrer Sterne
Wie Schmetterlinge weh'n?
Mein Spiegel in der Sonne
Wiegt Kinder in der Nacht:
Die übergroße Wonne,
So traurig, und so sacht…
Ich lass mir wohl erlauben,
In Wogen in der Bucht,
Den Klang der jüng'ren Kalben
Zerlindern, meine Wucht.

[T W E N T Y - F I V E]

Crown of Flowers

She's sworn to felicity,
Roses in bed,
Reborn electricity
Poses in stead
Just how Jeannie's calling him
Up and away:
The dream of her stalling gymkhana—
To pray a round of erotic stems
Facing his love,
In fields of stratagems:
Harvest her glove,
Recover from yonder loss—
Leave left behind
Scars, stars, and a rugged cross
Life loses to find.

[TWENTY-SIX]

Rainbow-Eye

If dreams are boats, you'll hear him bark,
Lest ebbtides take control:
For vessels are like women—hark,
Just listen to their shoal!

They swim below, as though to show
Their waters may bestow
More Fahrenheit than might a kite
That flows from go to woe—

And grows to glow, a narrow bow
Is no match for his coals
One Norseman tries to overthrow
In studies cooked by holes...

Who put him there? He's innocent,
Remultiplied by hurt:
Love would assert a winner meant
Small pleasure's inner spurt!

[TWENTY-SEVEN]
One Knight Only

Community of sexes—God,
Hey, wherefore not bless love?
If that's a jolly nexus, odd
Is it for dreaming of?

So, spare the prejudicial pain:
The man, the rich, the white—
The Christian on his monoplane
Whose hetero is right!

You leap to false delusions, yes,
You point to three-point stars:
Howbeit my conclusions, bless
Me, blinded by Papa's,

Is *Weltanschauung* seeing what
Seems more or less secure—
Until six shiny wheels' plot
Turns woodwork to manure!

[TWENTY-EIGHT]

Two Voices

Once or twice upon a chime
They bound together books,
Until the time it was a crime
To sew together looks!

And once or thrice these books were lent
Ex libris to a friend,
To be, or not to be exempt
From learning—but depend,

Occasions found these archetypes
Arranged on shelves, for more
To dust them off, with hurt or hype's
Sore second-hand rapport…

Read them all! Devour whole
The knowledge of mankind!
Oops, I did too, and truth I stole—
No wonder I resigned!

[TWENTY-NINE]

Dumbo The Cat

Ladies, laddies, guys and gals,
The rationale for God
To plough the planet, beaux and belles
Expelled—they shake and nod...

Where is my plumage, pelican?
And where my tuna? Play,
My darling, where your belly-span
And fur makes night of day!

I see the plodders, and my soul
Regurgitates their plum
Expulsion from the Golden Bowl,
But now I hear the dumb

Pronounce me crazy, feed me bread
Like chickenfeed, because
They do not think I ever said
How ignorant I was.

[THIRTY]

Rich Her Lime

Rich her lemon, rich her lime,
Rich her Roma, too:
To get together, make a prime—
Two sets of twins another time,
As if she only knew!

Hope is never lost until
They put you in a box—
They put you down, so sweetly spill
Red roses, or a porta-grill
To hide your lack of locks!

But till the day I die, I live
To know that inner joy—
Much better to receive than give,
Will do the job a very sieve
Lent humankind a boy.

[THIRTY-ONE]

Crowns

Alive, and living, till we're not—
Aromas in the living sods,
Whose grass is given unto pot—
The inners changing into gods,
Whom rooms conceded—tell me what
I do, at home, in empty pods…

Wires are too thick to break,
For I am weak, and one to see
Through slats in windows, ere I wake
Is frowned upon—if you were me,
You'd tie my history to a stake
And keep me on it, mercifully

Contending sonnets speak of love,
And, drawing breath, give mine reprieve…

[THIRTY-TWO]

Bridge

I lay me, sacramentally,
On linen clothing down—
Never thinking, sensually,
Spirit green and brown
Is watching, evidentially
Love would come to town!

Too stubborn to remember when
Two eyebrows can be seen
Above the flicker of a wren
So clear, concise, so clean,
I flew the coop, my hopes to wean
On quite another scene…

There *is* a chance, one chance remains
To live, in love, too true—she deigns!

[THIRTY-THREE]
Communion

Extraordinheiress to the throne,
In love with truth and light,
Might realise a king's a loan,
Thee loving through the night—
For fantasies cannot postpone,
Nor grey shall blacken white!

The Sun arose, still water wet
And drying out the sea,
Excluding fishes—let us let
Them flounder, soon to be
Exotic angel fish we met
In all tranquillity…

Two lovebirds in a cotton cage
Will lie on woollen wads, too sage
To peck at bread, once seed too few
To leave them empty, way too true!

[THIRTY-FOUR]

Flower

God let the goldfish down the stream
Through foreign windows ope—
Thy vision, knowledge, through a dream,
With just sufficient rope,
Wakes up on Planet Earth, a meme
For once an antelope…

Divinity, thy breastplate is
Thy shield for the fight:
My sword put patient, best-wait-whiz
Intoxications right

Before the setting of the Sun
Which rises into day—
The night will see the battle won
From yester in a fray

Till morrows wake without, and we
Shall see the seedling bud
Beneath the starry canopy
Of fire, stone, and mud.

[THIRTY-FIVE]

Picnic

Axe Shaun, phiz Ed, sac Jack, fool Phil—
If you've got nuts to give,
Alicia, be my bushy hill,
And I can be your spiv!

Before you fall, here comes the Sun,
And all things pass away:
It's time to do the sums, the fun,
Forever and a day,

Is old and dry, with paint that cracks,
But cosier than warm:
If someone cleans your ceiling wax,
You'll need no other swarm

To pollinate, and thicken soup
To feast on for your good
Impatience for his chicken coop—
The clearing in her wood.

[THIRTY-SIX]

Prints

Division can belong,
Hiatus is a gap
To right a little wrong
For Venus and her trap—

A sonnet for a song,
As wisdom takes a nap,
Lest tugger be a nong
And come up short, a lap
Along a swimming pool—
Well, sometimes it'll sap
The lover in tomorrow's fool
And chip a little chap
Who's gotten older, tends to drool
For telling too much—zap!

Herodotus, don't go to war
For fortune or for fame:
Check history, that's what it's for—
Play Chess, to kill and maim!

[THIRTY-SEVEN]

To The Max

For further dust a crispy crust
Would bring me to my knees—
We're mammals with a lust that must
Initiate with please—

Still, one there was so innocent
Who, very good with words,
Could not enunciate a scent
Nor weigh nocturnal curds:

So, ignorance would win the day,
As every girl would scram
To see the other tradies lay
Their holsters in a dam—
And mass debates, years seven, eight,
Flew lightly over head
Until a chance occasion, late
At one, or two, in bed,
Did move the earth beneath his feet,
Not even holding on:
The eagle and the hawk would meet,
To prove all hope was gone.

[THIRTY-EIGHT]

Very Clear

You cannot tell a Lutheran
That Jesus Christ is God—
But you can ride my scooter, Ann,
And sock it to my rod!

A little time before I die,
A little less to do—
I'd have mine over easy, why,
That's how you like 'm too!

We'll eat a little sunshine, on
The streets without our names:
I don't know Checkers—are you fond
Of other endings, games

Just you and I came home alone
To be together with?
We'll pay lip service to the phone—
The one you tether with!

[THIRTY-NINE]

Extended Dance Mix

I am who I am, but one of us just wasn't good enough:
A ram bore a lamb, intermission too tough…
When I was so small, thought I with a smile—
And it didn't appal, nor come back for a while—
What if I was the Lord, of whom they all spoke,
In whom spirit soared, in whom majesty woke?
But the best-looking boy turned into a crab,
For where is the joy to get gifts for the gab,
When the tiger's Leroy, and you're up for the tab?
So, I paid all the bills when I knocked at her door,
When, despite all the pills, recognition was poor:
But I waddled along, and I ducked on a hunch,
Till the jealous and wrong beat my soul to the punch,
And my friends the police put the sting in my tail,
For to give me the peace, seven seconds travail,
But not as the end—if I marched into Hell,
The Dragon's no friend, and the Beast, I could tell,
Was laughing inside the cold place where a heart
Thought victory his—I woke up with a start…

[F O R T Y]

Bobby-Pins

Love, my love is writ—I care
That only words may be too few:
To think on thee, of thee I stare
Into the morrow's dawning dew.

A blackbird spake, the snake is wan,
And in this mirror's even clay
A woman whom I wish upon
Appropriates what's left to say:

I love thee—if I wait too long
To speak three words through teeth and lips,
The Sun will settle all along
The bobby-pins and paperclips—

To leave my tongue, there burièd,
No words to exit from—
No words to ask thee to be wed,
So able, and so dumb.

[FORTY-ONE]

Every Dream

Every dream I never had
Is come, to be with you—
My sonnets, on a virgin pad,
Accompanied, ensue:

My greatest hope, this day to be
Inside, and hear you cry—
Five droplets from a canopy
Mere wishing well the sky—

To see your face, your locks, your lips,
Your lowerings of lash,
Till bodies, bountied, hands on hips,
Return our dust to ash—

The place I want to show the love
You're merging with my soul,
Together, got you, how above
You are to fish and roll!

[FORTY-TWO]
The Lee-Flower

She, the cat, the mother, friendliness
To nestle in my heart
Being broken, was descending
Blest into my apple cart—

With wisps of woken winter warmth
Which won the willow's breeze—
Eleventh hour's brave adornment
To my chalk and cheese!

Do let regret me not forget
The flower here this day,
The earth that makes her petals wet
Is glistening—as clay

Surrounds our perpendiculars
And, rising into groves
Of terracotta sickles, stars
With laughter, and with love.

[FORTY-THREE]

Tired

In recompense your innocence forgave you half a shot:
  You fell to Hell, benevolence abandoned, left to rot:
Son, Heaven's overrated, that's the first mistake in Chess,
  But you've investigated brats, like brethren in a mess…
    Who is this Holy Spirit, mate? Fecundity's a dove?
And who's the God you irritate to love, who loves to love
  You? David got deposed, exposing love to lactic maids
Admitting Moses, born to smite in callous hit parades…
    Okay, another *précis* here, your lacking willing one
Commanding *prima facie*, dear, the dark side of the Son:
Who came to conquer everything, all but a second death,
  As, marching into suffering's hot cauldron in *Macbeth*,
    Was bold as gold: To entertain eternity down there,
Your saving grace bereft of gain got cleaned up in despair
Forgone for nanoseconds—hey, Hashem'd let you drown!
  If ego's hopping reckons, hell, the Evil One's a clown,
    As gnashing teeth beweep a sickle twisting as you shout,
A screw's as loose as fur you burn, give up on getting out!
  That Satan is a lover—no? Leave tips for Frankenstein:
  A sister for a mother, grow to honour—heart and vine!

[FORTY-FOUR]

Lacking Jak

I wish upon your star at night—
Long time, no see, tis true—
And, bathing in nocturnal light,
I hope it touches you.

I breathe your air—and if you aren't
Molecular and free,
It seems the birds that chirp and chant
Must sing in spite of me.

Your eyes caress the shaking leaves
Of summertime beyond
How fervently the breeze believes
Of thee I must be fond.

[FORTY-FIVE]

Lynda

Tranquil, tender, hot and cool—
To chase an ember, as a rule,
And fan the flames within our park,
Is work for love's light in the dark!

How is it you make calm the storm?
Not far from you I feel warm,
To find your for-me-fancy form
Felicitous—as though a dorm

Were not more than a smile away:
The twinkle in your cosmic ray
Is starshine white and red and grey
On Checker boards, to my dismay…

The curtain closes—no-one claps,
A testimony's done, perhaps
Made lovely, finding time for two's
Soul sister notes inside peruse!

[F O R T Y · S I X]

Endeavour

Ships we saw, aye captain, more
Than sands on rocks where seeds
Evoke the yoke of Satan's claw—
Vexatious, vicious screeds
Entrusting gusts to scatter spoor
Nefarious as weeds!

Mendacity's admixture—now
Apocalyptic hues
Rip Batman down—biff, bam, kapow—
To put us in his shoes,
In saying you're not welcome: ciao,
Nobody wanted youse!

To care, or not to care about
Olivia—all lies
Stand out, as if you were to shout
Seduction to the skies'
Exotic chemistry: a lout
Refuted, gnashes, cries.

[FORTY-SEVEN]

The One

Who, reading lines and strokes,
To come, and is, applauds,
Will be my rain and shining cloaks—
The rainbow she affords…

Tremble, leaves, before the storm
Becomes a breeze again—
The fire in my heart keeps warm
The beauty and the pain…

Art thou not near? A lonesome tear
Will be not mine to breed:
So, call me handsome—call me seer,
And thou hast cause to bleed!

[FORTY-EIGHT]

Eternity's Pair

She saved my life, for in the light
The White Queen rules the board!
Caïssa—Mrs Taylor, right?
So swift, my carpet soared
From Avalon, to be with thee,
The one I could afford—
For fearing God sufficiently's
A necessary chord…

Come quietly, you're thirty still,
I may be thirty-one—
If I, to quill love's holy will,
Saw loss, where there was none,

Slip, svelte, so savvy, sweet as trust,
As hope, as longing first
Rewards high skies with angel dust,
Just loving is my thirst!

[FORTY-NINE]

Santa Maria

So calm, creative, *comme il faut,*
More sunshine than it takes
To keep this Earth more high than low—
As, *süt a nap,* it bakes!

Look what they've done to your song, Love—
They treat it as a tray:
I thank thee, God, thy will above
Is with us, day by day!

Still, just to get the Garden back
Before the Golden Bowl,
Once blue and green and brown, is black
As cherry for the foal

With nowhere left to grow and prance,
With no-one left to mourn—
Absentia we'd sew and dance
Before the world was born!

[F I F T Y]

Ruth

Too true! I rue, for fools like me
Who play a card, must let it lie:
Impossible to stand—if she
Left Love intact, and Hope to cry,
I'd live again—don't ask me why!

Goodbye to fire, O my heart,
You heat in hope, yet want to not—
To love is when your zeal's art
Has got a rose in every plot
In every garden God forgot...

I guess you'd never know a rope's
Erotic too—lest I remind
How fledgling Faith has got the Pope's
Frank imprimatur, Love resigned
On cue, as troubadours unwind
In cliques of keen, collusive chords,
Regretting Pawn moves, crossing swords,
To seize the day the night rewards
With Lords in hordes—too many words!